# This book belongs to

Austin

# MY MAGIC TREE HOUSE® JOURNAL

## MARY POPE OSBORNE, NATALIE POPE BOYCE, AND YOU!

(YOUR NAME HERE)

### ILLUSTRATED BY SAL MURDOCCA

A STEPPING STONE BOOK™

Random House 🏠 New York

Library of Congress Control Number: 2013940600
ISBN: 978-0-385-37505-4

MANUFACTURED IN CHINA
10 9 8 7 6 5 4 3 2 1

We really love to explore! We're always discovering new things in Frog Creek and in our travels all over the world. We keep track of what we discover in our journals. Now we want to share a special journal with you. We'll tell you all about us if you'll tell us all about you—we promise. This journal is about your world, your town, your own backyard . . . and you! When you've finished writing in it, stop by MagicTreeHouse.com to unlock even more journal activities. Check the end of the book for information.

Turn the page so we can begin!

THIS WAY

You don't have to go far away to find fun places to explore! We don't even have to go any farther than our own backyard. We can find lots of cool animals, plants, and bugs right by our house in Frog Creek. How about you?

You can use the stickers to decorate your pages or to mark your favorite things!

# Animals in Our Backyard

squirrels

Lumbricidae (Bet you have at least one in
    your backyard . . . but what is it? Hint:
    robins love them!)

snails

moles

crows

cardinals

robins

frogs . . . of course!

rabbits

chipmunks

Did you know that crows are the
smartest birds in the United States?

Draw or attach pictures of the animals you see in your backyard.

Wow! Great picture!

# Animals in Your Backyard

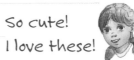

So cute!
I love these!

# Bugs and Spiders in Our Backyard

ants

bees

mosquitoes

butterflies

houseflies

grasshoppers

moths

praying mantises

garden spiders

horseflies

**Houseflies beat their wings 200 or more times a second!**

Jack took this.
Great photo, Jack!

There are 20,000
different types of bees.

Ants get information by
touching each other's antennae.

# Bugs and Spiders
# in Your Backyard

_____

_____

_____

_____

_____

_____

_____

_____

_____

A magnifying
glass is great
for getting a
close-up view!

# Your Favorite Butterfly

Our favorite butterfly is the monarch. They fly south 2,500 miles or more in the winter. You can find lots of butterfly pictures online or in books. Draw your favorite kind of butterfly and write down two cool facts about it.

# Plants in Our Backyard

**Dandelion seeds can travel up to 500 miles in the wind!**

grass

dandelions

violets

clovers

daisies

ferns

maple tree

pine tree

oak tree

apple tree

# Plants in Your Backyard

# Stars in Our Backyard

We love looking at the stars on a summer night. Remember when we had to wear space suits on the moon? You don't need them in your backyard!

We're not astronomers with powerful telescopes. We've seen these stars, planets, and constellations just by looking up!

Sirius, also known as the Dog Star

Polaris, or the North Star

Venus, second planet from the sun and
   brightest object in the night sky

Big Dipper

Orion's Belt

# Stars in Your Backyard

What about you? Step outside on a really dark night when there isn't any moonlight or many clouds. Can you find the Big Dipper? What else?

# Our Nature Hike

We really like to hike! We put all the things we need in our backpacks. Remember how Leonardo da Vinci said, "Just open your eyes and look around"? That's the way we see animals and interesting plants that we might have missed otherwise.

This is what we like to take with us for a hike:

notebooks

pencils

sunscreen

someone older who knows the trail!

tree and wildflower guide

bird guide

water

binoculars

Band-Aids

magnifying glass

camera

bug spray

Don't forget a snack!

# Your Nature Hike

What about you? If you were going on a nature hike on a spring day, what would you pack? Remember, be safe! Always ask permission or go with an adult.

# Scavenger Hunts for All Seasons

When we explore our neighborhood, we find different things in winter, spring, summer, and fall.

Have you ever been on a scavenger hunt? Challenge yourself—or get together a group of friends—to find all the things on our lists. If some are too hard to find or just don't exist in your area, you can use the spaces below our lists to come up with your own things. When you find something, put a check mark next to it.

# Winter Scavenger Hunt

pine needles ☐

icicle ☐

brown leaf ☐

ice-covered branch ☐

squirrel tracks ☐

bird tracks ☐

birds at a feeder ☐

tall dried grasses ☐

piles of snow ☐

ice-covered ponds or lakes ☐

snowman ☐

_____ ☐

_____ ☐

_____ ☐

Turn the page to check out other
seasons for more scavenger hunts!

# Spring Scavenger Hunt

- [ ] pussy willows
- [ ] buds on branch
- [ ] bluets
- [ ] crocuses
- [ ] baby rabbits
- [ ] robins
- [ ] sounds of frogs
- [ ] daffodils
- [ ] apple blossoms
- [ ] flocks of geese returning
- [ ] lots of singing birds
- [ ] _____
- [ ] _____
- [ ] _____

Bluets are very light blue spring flowers.

We don't mind rainy spring days. They make the flowers and trees bloom and grow. Sometimes the rains give us beautiful rainbows. What do you like best about spring?

# Summer Scavenger Hunt

Summer days seem to last forever. A scavenger hunt can break up a long, lazy day.

- ☐ maple tree leaf
- ☐ moss
- ☐ dandelions
- ☐ fern leaf
- ☐ black-eyed Susans
- ☐ clovers . . . Maybe you can find a four-leaf clover?
- ☐ green pinecone
- ☐ bark
- ☐ feather
- ☐ smooth gray rock
- ☐ _____
- ☐ _____
- ☐ _____

The tree house is nice and shady on a hot day.
What are some ways you stay cool in the heat?

_____

_____

_____

_____

_____

_____

_____

_____

# Fall Scavenger Hunt

- ☐ yellow leaf
- ☐ orange leaf
- ☐ red leaf
- ☐ woolly bear
- ☐ maple seed
- ☐ milkweed pod
- ☐ apples
- ☐ pumpkins
- ☐ goldenrod
- ☐ acorn
- ☐ _____
- ☐ _____
- ☐ _____

Woolly bear caterpillars turn into tiger moths in the spring.

Draw or attach pictures of things you found or pictures of you and your friends on your scavenger hunts!

Different seasons give us different ways to have fun. How do you have fun in each of them?

# Winter

 I love to sled in the winter. You too?

# Spring

 Really? I like that, too!

# Summer

We love to swim!

# Fall

Soccer season in Frog Creek!

# Frog Creek ... and Your Town

We really love Frog Creek! It's a small place, but it's full of great things. Is your town anything like ours? Or maybe you live in a big city, with lots of tall buildings and wonderful museums. We love exploring all kinds of towns and cities. Each of them is different and each has fun things to do.

## Where you live:

|  | small town | big city | medium-sized town |
|---|---|---|---|
| Frog Creek | ✓ | | |
| Where you live | | | |

## Ways you get around town:

|  | bike | walk | car | train | bus |
|---|---|---|---|---|---|
|  | ✓ | ✓ | ✓ | | ✓ |
|  | | | | | |

## What's the land like?

| woods | fields | hills | beach | mountains | desert |
|---|---|---|---|---|---|
| ✓ | ✓ | ✓ | | | |
| | | | | | |

## What's the weather like?

|  | four seasons | hot | very cold | always rainy |
|---|---|---|---|---|
|  | ✓ | | | |
|  | | | | |

Hilo, Hawaii, is the rainiest city in the United States.

# Buildings in Frog Creek

our house

school

post office

fire station

town hall

grocery store

police station

hospital

ice cream shop

library

# Buildings in Your Town

_____

_____

_____

_____

_____

_____

_____

_____

_____

_____

_____

_____

Your town sounds so cool!

# Our Favorite Places
## in Frog Creek

Frog Creek woods

public library

soccer field at school

bakery with yummy cookies

sledding hill near our house

public swimming pool

bench on Main Street, where we sit with friends

theater on Main Street, where we see plays

town lake, where we have picnics

# Your Favorite Places
# in Your Town

_____

_____

_____

_____

_____

_____

Draw or attach a picture of your very favorite place in your town.

# Jobs in Frog Creek

Even in a small town like Frog Creek, there are lots of different jobs. Here are some people we've seen around town:

teacher

librarian (not Morgan!)

police officer

firefighter

mayor

doctor

grocery store clerk

auto mechanic

school bus driver

We've seen meteorologists on TV!

# Jobs in Your Town

What jobs do you see people doing in your town?

_____

_____

_____

_____

_____

_____

What do you want to be when you grow up?
Why? (Really think about it!)

_____

_____

_____

_____

_____

_____

# The Mayor

Citizens in almost every town or city vote for people to run their town. The mayor is the head of most towns. Mayors do lots of things, like making sure the streets and parks are clean and that the town has laws to keep people safe.

The mayor's office is usually at city hall or town hall. When people want things changed, they often write to the mayor with their ideas. Sometimes the mayor will write back!

Write a letter to your mayor. Tell him or her what you think needs improving or what you like in your town. (If your mayor is doing a good job, say "thank you!")

Date:

Dear Mayor _____ ,

_____

_____

_____

_____

_____

_____

_____

_____

Sincerely,

_____
your signature

# Our Most Exciting Day

The most exciting day for us in Frog Creek was when we discovered the tree house. Remember how we climbed up a rope ladder and found a room full of books? One was about dinosaurs. Jack pointed at a picture in the book. He wished we could go there. Next the wind started to blow. And then the tree house began to spin ... faster and faster. That was the day in Frog Creek when all our incredible adventures began!

Now tell us something exciting that happened in your town!

# Your Most Exciting Day

It's your turn! What's the most exciting thing that's ever happened to you in your town?

The most exciting thing that's ever

happened in _____ was

when _____

_____

_____

_____

_____

_____

_____

_____

_____

_____

_____

Wow! Draw us a picture of that!

# Plan Your Dream Town

Pretend you're a city planner. Draw a map of the buildings and parks your town would need. Would you have a skateboard park? Bike trails? Playgrounds? Show where you think the police station, hospital, and fire station should be. Would you like a lot of ice cream shops and restaurants? It's your town . . . make it the way you want!

# Books!

Your town library has some great books, and best of all, they're free! What are your favorite books? Put your very favorite at the top of the list.

 I love books that are full of new things to learn!

My favorite books are:

Draw a scene from one of your favorite books.

I really love exciting adventure books!

# Your School

If you're like us, one building you spend a lot of time in is your school. What does it look like? Draw a picture. You might want to draw yourself with your friends or standing beside your teacher or principal. You can add labels for the name of your school and for any of the people in the picture.

# Your School Day

Tell us about your day!

_____

I get up at _____

Then I _____

_____

We do that, too!

_____

I leave for school at _____

When I get to school, the first thing I do is

_____

_____

My favorite part of the

day is _____

_____

I get out of school at

_____

# Your Classroom

What does your classroom look like? Draw us a map!

Cool room!

# Best and Worst at School

What was the best thing that happened in your school this year?

What was the worst thing?

# Reading Buddies

In our school, we have a reading buddies program. An older kid pairs up with a younger kid, and they read together. This is a terrific way for younger kids to become great readers. And it feels good for the older buddies to help their young buddies discover a new love of reading.

Does your school, library, or bookstore have a reading buddies program? If not, you can always find a reading buddy on your own. If you're just beginning to read or ready to start, maybe you have an older relative or neighbor or friend who would like to read with you. If you're already a good reader, why not share your love of reading with someone younger? It's fun!

Be sure to pick out a book both you and your buddy will enjoy. Then you can fill out the next journal page together.

# Your Reading Buddy Journal

Your name _____

Your buddy's name _____

Title _____

Did you like the book? ___ yes ___ no

Did your buddy like the book? ___ yes ___ no

What was your favorite part?

_____

_____

_____

What was your buddy's favorite part?

_____

_____

_____

Would you read with a buddy again?

___ yes ___ no

Would your buddy read with a buddy
again? ___ yes ___ no

# Our Favorite Sport

After school, we play soccer. It's our favorite sport to play and to watch. The magic tree house took us to Mexico in 1970 to see the World Cup. What a day that was!

# Your Favorite Sport

Do you play any sports? Which ones?

What's your favorite sport?

Draw or attach a picture of you playing your favorite sport.

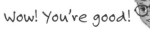

Wow! You're good!

# Tree House Travels

We've been all over the world—and even to the moon! We've had missions on every continent, including Antarctica.

# Places We've Been

Paris New York City Baghdad Venice Hawaii African savannah United States Pacific Ocean Atlantic Ocean Florence Western Japan Amazon England Egypt Caribbean Sea Swiss Alps New Orleans China Austria Antarctica San Francisco Congo Arctic Pompeii Ireland Australia India Greece Great Plains Plymouth Mexico

# Map of the Places We've Been in the Magic Tree House

Let's put that on the map! We've put dots on this map to show where we've been in the world.

·North Pole

Irela

Paris, France·

Venice, Italy—

Florence, Ital
Pompeii, Italy—

Western
United States—

North
America

Massachusetts
New York City

San Francisco—

·Pacific Ocean

Atlantic
Ocean

Hawaii

Mexico—

·Caribbean Sea

New Orleans

South
America

Amazon rain
forest

·Antarctic

Swiss Alps
Austria
England
Europe
Asia
Japan
China
Africa
Greece
India
Baghdad, Iraq
Egypt
African savannah
Congo
Australia

THIS WAY

Turn the page to tell us about your travels!

It's your turn! Where have you been? What's the number one place you'd like to go?

Draw or attach a copy of your passport picture here, or draw a place you would like to visit.

Remember, if you travel to another country, don't forget your passport!

# Places You've Been and Places You'd Like to Go

Use the stickers to highlight your favorites.

# Map of Places You've Been and Places You'd Like to Go

Put a dot on the map for places you've been and places you'd like to go.

Europe

Asia

Africa

Australia

These are great places!

# Time Travel

Travel through time
with Jack and Annie!

If you could travel to another time, when would it be?

I would like to go back to the time when

_____

_____

_____

_____

_____

_____

_____

Draw or attach pictures of what you would
have seen during this time.

Draw a picture of yourself in the kind of clothes
you would have worn.

# At the Beach

One of our favorite places to travel to is the ocean. Sure, we love to play in the waves and build sand castles and bury each other in the sand, but we also like to explore. There's so much you can see at the beach, from dolphins leaping out of the water to the tiniest brine shrimp and other animals living in tide pools.

Did you know that dunes and dune grass protect the shore from flooding?

Yes! And did you know that if all the salt in the ocean wa spread on the land, it would b 500 feet thick—as high as a forty-story building?

# What We Found at the Beach

scallop shell

skate egg sac

seaweed

sand dollar

clamshell

sand crab

driftwood

sea glass

plastic milk carton! (Yuck!)

# At the Beach

Do you have a favorite beach?

_____

_____

Do you have to travel far to get there?

_____

_____

Where is it?

_____

_____

# What You Found at the Beach

Did you know that beach sand is really rocks that have been ground up very fine by the sea?

# Packing for the Beach

When you're going on a beach trip, try to pack what you need. To make sure we're ready, we take our bathing suits, of course. But there are lots of other things to think about as well.

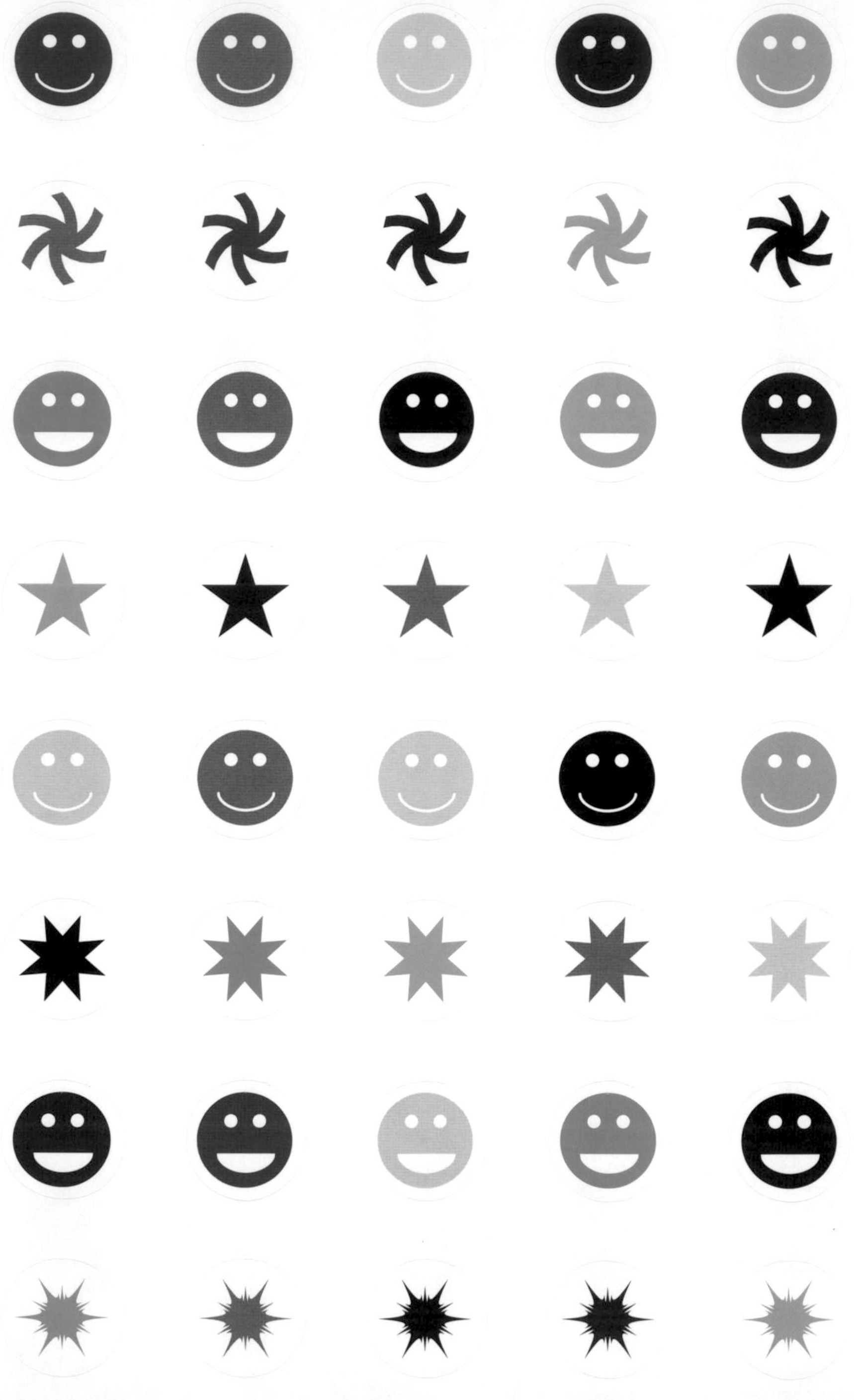

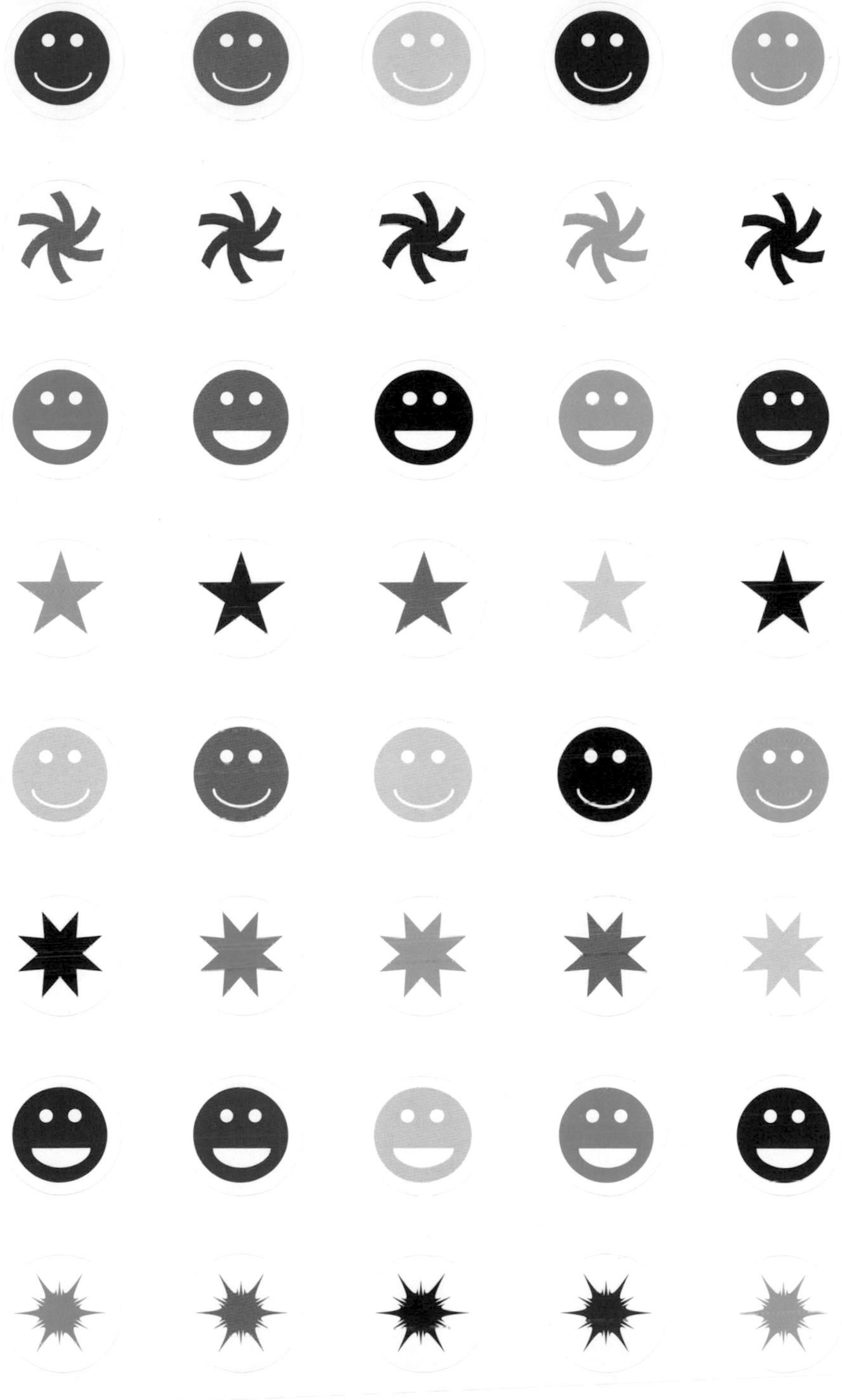

What would you pack to take to the beach?
(Not gloves and coats!)

Don't forget a hat!

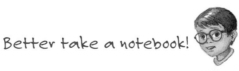
Better take a notebook!

# Packing for a Ski Trip

We love skiing. Did you know that people skied in cold countries over 5,000 years ago? They used handmade wooden skis to travel over the snow.

We know it'll be cold on the ski slopes, so we pack warm clothes.

Afterward we really enjoy a cup of good hot cocoa!

# What would you take on a ski trip?

Brrrr . . . Of course you'll need warm clothes, hats, and gloves!

Don't forget the marshmallows for the cocoa!

# Packing for More Trips

What about your list of places you'd like to go? Think of one and what you'd need to bring with you. Where are you going? What do you need to pack?

# Draw pictures of everything you'd pack!

# Desert Island

If we were stranded on a desert island, we would want lots of books to read. And notebooks and pencils to record our adventures . . . and maybe some colored pencils for drawing.

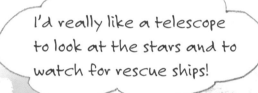

I'd really like a telescope to look at the stars and to watch for rescue ships!

Pretend you'll be stranded on an island for two weeks. You can take only six things to have fun with. What would they be?

Wow! Cool!

# Famous Places We've Seen

On our trips in the magic tree house, we've seen some of the most famous places in the world.

| **What?** | **Where?** |
|---|---|
| Basilica di Santa Maria del Fiore | Florence, Italy |
| Empire State Building | New York City |
| Eiffel Tower | Paris, France |
| Pyramids | Egypt |
| Globe Theater | London, England |
| Pompeii | Italy |
| White House | Washington, D.C. |
| ancient Olympic stadium | Olympia, Greece |
| summer palace | Vienna, Austria |
| French Quarter | New Orleans, Louisiana |

# Famous Places
# You've Seen

What about you? What are some famous places you've seen?

| What? | Where? |
| --- | --- |
| | |
| | |
| | |
| | |

What are some famous places you'd like to see?

| What? | Where? |
| --- | --- |
| | |
| | |
| | |
| | |

Draw or attach pictures of some of your favorite landmarks.

Here are two blank pages, just for you. Use these to write anything you want!

# Holidays

We've celebrated all kinds of holidays all over the world. We were in New Orleans for All Saints' Day and Venice for Winter Carnival. We spent Christmas in Camelot. And we even got to celebrate Thanksgiving in Plymouth, Massachusetts!

What is your favorite family holiday?

_____

_____

Why do you celebrate this day?

_____

_____

Who celebrates with you?

_____

_____

What special foods do you eat?

_____

_____

# Your Birthday

What day is your birthday?

My birthday is:

_____

Did you know that in Brazil, birthday kids eat candies shaped like fruits and vegetables?

And in India, children eat a kind of rice pudding instead of cake? Birthdays are different for kids everywhere! Celebrate!

# Plan Your Perfect
# Birthday Party

Guests:

_____    _____

_____    _____

_____    _____

_____    _____

_____    _____

What would you eat?

What would you do?

Where would you have it?

What would you wear?

Would you promise to thank everyone?

YES! (There is no other answer!)

# Our Best Friends

| Favorite friends: | What is special about them? |
|---|---|
| Teddy | Teddy is funny and |
| | surprising. Remember all the |
| | times he's helped us? |
| | |
| Kathleen | Kathleen is kind, brave, |
| | and really friendly. |
| | She's a great friend! |
| | |
| | |
| | |
| | |

We want to hear about your friends! Turn
the page to tell us all about them!

THIS WAY

# Your Best Friends

Draw or attach pictures of your friends here.

| Favorite friends: | What is special about them? |
| --- | --- |
|  |  |
|  |  |
|  |  |
|  |  |
|  |  |
|  |  |
|  |  |
|  |  |
|  |  |
|  |  |
|  |  |
|  |  |
|  |  |
|  |  |
|  |  |
|  |  |

# Families

Annie and I laugh a lot and like to spend time together. Not all families are the same, but every family has people who care for each other. We bet you have lots of great people in your family!

# Your Family

Who are the people in your family, and what are they like?

**Name:**                    **Description:**

_____      _____

_____      _____

_____      _____

_____      _____

_____      _____

_____      _____

Draw or attach pictures of some of the people in your family.

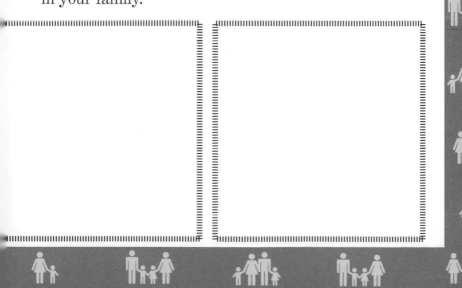

# What Makes Us Happy

Lots of things make us happy, like going on family trips, reading on a rainy day, and laughing with our friends.

Other things that make us happy:

reading great adventure stories

learning new facts

hanging out with Teddy and Kathleen

riding our bikes

visiting with our grandparents

making each other laugh

playing soccer

swimming in the ocean

performing magic tricks

getting to know great dogs and

taking care of animals like

hamsters, gerbils, turtles,

fish, kittens, parakeets,

and many more!

# What makes you happy—really, really happy?

Draw or attach pictures of some of the things
you listed.

# Things That Make Us Laugh

funny-sounding food, like squash

and fried stinky tofu

wearing pointy slippers

getting knocked down and licked

by a Saint Bernard

trying to catch eels with our

bare hands

dancing the hula

Oh, man! I looked silly in this!

# Things That Make You Laugh

What about you? What tickles your funny bone?

_____

_____

_____

_____

_____

_____

Oh, wow! You <u>have</u> to show us a picture of that!

# Things That
# Really Bug Us

millions of army ants

hairy spiders bigger than Jack

disease-carrying mosquitoes on the Nile

rats and bats in a haunted house

cobras and boa constrictors

yelping jackals

hungry hyenas

What really bugs you? Your top ten!

# Our Favorite Animals

We've met these great animals and really love them:

pandas

emperor penguins

Saint Bernards

dolphins

gorillas

polar bears

mice

koalas

lions

a giant octopus

kangaroos

**A baby kangaroo is called a <u>joey</u>.**

# What are your top ten favorite animals?

_____

_____

_____

_____

_____

_____

This animal
is amazing!

_____

_____

_____

# Be Your Favorite Animal!

If you could be one of your favorite animals for twenty-four hours, which one would you be? How would you act? What would your habitat be? What would you eat? How would you behave? We have lots of questions. Tell us some great facts!

Draw or attach a picture of the animal you choose.

What animal would you like to be?

If I were a _____

I would live _____

I would eat _____

My coloring would be _____

I would spend my day _____

_____

My skin or fur would be _____

The most interesting fact about me is

_____

Am I a fast mover or a slow mover? _____

I sleep _____ hours a day.

Am I an endangered species? ___ yes ___ no

What I like best about myself:

_____

_____

_____

_____

# Baby Animals We've Saved

On our travels, we've helped lots of animals, including some adorable babies. Here are some of the baby animals we've saved:

Sunset, a mustang colt

Roly and Poly, panda cubs

Joey, a baby kangaroo

Bu-bu, a baby gorilla

Penny, a baby penguin

Koku, a baby baboon

# Baby Animals
# You'd Like to Save

What baby animals would you most like to rescue if you could?

# Pets

If you could have any animal for a pet, what would it be? Why?

Remember Peanut the mouse?

Do you really have any pets? If so, draw us a picture and tell us all about them. Do your pets do funny things? What are their names?

I have _____

_____

_____

Their names are

_____

_____

I love them because _____

_____

The worst thing they ever did was _____

_____

The funniest thing they ever did was _____

_____

My pet eats a lot. ___ yes ___ no

My pet needs to go on a diet. ___ yes ___ no

My pet likes to cuddle. ___ yes ___ no

My pet has eaten my homework. ___ yes ___ no

# The Amazing Inventor

In *Monday with a Mad Genius*, we met Leonardo da Vinci, the great artist and inventor. He thought up the most amazing things, like a flying machine called the Great Bird! Leonardo kept notebooks full of ideas for his inventions.

# Your Amazing Invention

Draw a cool invention. It can be anything!
Write about what it does.

_____

_____

_____

_____

_____

# Our Favorite Ways to Get Around

Why walk or ride the bus when you could travel in a magic tree house? We've used all kinds of magical transportation on our missions. Here are some of our favorites:

unicorn

winged stag

flying lion

magic carpet

flying two-seater bicycle

# Your Favorite Way to Get Around

What if you could use any kind of transportation your imagination dreamed up? What would be your favorite way to get around?

Draw a picture of your magical transportation.

# Ghosts We've Met and Liked Along the Way

Some people are afraid of ghosts, but not us. (At least not much!) We've met so many nice ones. Here are some of our favorites:

dancing pirate ghosts

Egyptian ghost-queen

Ghosts of Past, Present, and Future

Lonesome Luke, a piano player in a

   ghost town

a ghostly girl spinning and ghostly boys

   playing chess in an ancient castle

# Ghosts You'd Like to Meet

What ghosts would you make friends with if you could?

_____

_____

_____

_____

_____

_____

# Some of the Times We Were Really Scared

We've been in very scary situations on our adventures. Here are some of the scariest:

hiding from a samurai warrior in old Japan

facing a sabertooth tiger in the Ice Age

visiting Pompeii when a volcano erupted

San Francisco earthquake of 1906

escaping a forest fire in Australia

running from a tiger in India

facing a pirate ghost in New Orleans

hiding from lions in Africa

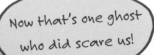

Now that's one ghost who did scare us!

# A Time You Were Really Scared

Tell us about a time when you were really afraid.

A time I was really scared was when _____

_____

_____

_____

_____

_____

_____

_____

_____

_____

# Your Awesome Ghost Story

We love scary stories, especially when we're sitting around a campfire at night. If we went on a sleepover or campout with you, what story would you tell? Use the next three pages to write the scariest, most awesome ghost story you can imagine.

_____ (Title)

Turn the page for more space for your story!

# Our Favorite Foods and Drinks

We love trying different foods. There are always new tastes to explore. Of course, we'll never stop loving our old favorites. Here are some of our all-time favorite foods and drinks:

lemonade

hot chocolate

coconut milk

dates

spaghetti

biscuits

sushi

corn bread

peanut butter and
    jelly sandwiches

honey tea

tacos

We had a little trouble with chopsticks at first!

# Your Favorite Foods and Drinks

What are some of your favorite things to eat and drink?

_____

_____

_____

What is the best thing you've ever eaten in your whole life?

Where did you have it? What did it look like? Did you ever have it again?

The best thing I ever ate was _____

_____

_____

_____

_____

_____

# Our Favorite Exclamations

Sometimes when we're excited or scared or amazed—like when we see a real, live leprechaun!—we just have to shout out. Here are some of our favorite exclamations:

Wow!

Oh, man!

Yippee!

Yay!

Oh, no!

Yuck!

Ahhh!

# Your Favorite Exclamations

What do you like to say when you shout out?

_____     _____

_____     _____

_____     _____

_____     _____

Draw a picture of yourself doing something exciting when you'd use these words.

ahhh!

oh, no!

wow!

yippee!

wow!

yuck!

yay!

oh, no!

ahhh!

oh, no!

wow!

# Mischief-Makers

In our adventures in the magic tree house, we've met our share of mischief-makers. They can be funny and frustrating, but we always love them in the end. Here are some of our favorite mischief-makers:

the pirates of the Caribbean

Koku, the baby baboon

Beauty and Cutie, two camels in Baghdad

Barry the Saint Bernard

# Mischief-Maker Poem

Have some fun! Write a poem about a mischief-maker—either one from our adventures, or one you make up from your imagination.

_____

(Title)

_____

_____

_____

_____

_____

_____

_____

_____

_____

_____

_____

# Missions

Merlin sends us on quests to do special things. Do you remember when we had to save Camelot and Venice and to find the secrets of happiness? Wow! It was so exciting!

Now it's your turn! We're inviting you on five special missions of your very own.

Dear _____,
Please accept the following missions. Write all about them so we know how they turned out.
—Jack and Annie

# Mission One

Your mission is to think of four things that will make the world a more peaceful place.

1. _____

_____

2. _____

_____

3. _____

_____

4. _____

_____

# **Mission Two**

Pretend your school doesn't allow anyone to laugh at anything! Your mission is to convince your teachers to change this rule.

I think laughing is important because _____

# Mission Three

You and your best friend are afraid of a bully at school. How can you stop this person?

I would start by _____

_____

_____

_____

_____

_____

_____

_____

_____

Bullies can be stopped!
Good ideas!

_____

_____

# Mission Four

A new kid has come into your class who doesn't wear cool clothes or speak much English and seems shy. Your mission is to help that kid feel welcome. What would you do?

To make a shy new kid feel welcome, I would

_____

_____

_____

_____

_____

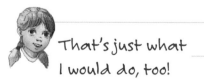

That's just what I would do, too!

_____

_____

# Mission Five

You are on a quest to look around in your class for someone you really admire. Your mission is to write him or her a letter saying why.

Dear _____ ,

I just want to tell you _____

_____

_____

_____

_____

_____

_____

_____

_____

_____

_____

# Photograph Credits

AlikeYou/Shutterstock (p. 10); Atovot/Shutterstock (p. 15); **Ruth Black/Shutterstock** (p. 82); **Javier Brosch/Shutterstock** (p. 57); **Vaidas Bucys/Shutterstock** (p. 63 bottom left); **goran cakmazovic/Shutterstock** (p. 7 middle); **ekler/Shutterstock** (pp. 54–55, 58–59, Antarctica only); **elenafoxly/Shutterstock** (pp. 118–119); **Marie C Fields/Shutterstock** (p. 63 bottom right); **Mike Flippo/Shutterstock** (p. 64); **Fotonium/Shutterstock** (p. 16 bottom left); **Eric Gevaert/Shutterstock** (p. 103); **Andre Goncalves/Shutterstock** (p. 7 top); **steven r. hendricks/Shutterstock** (p. 18 bottom); **Sonny Hudson/Shutterstock** (p. 20 top); **ildogesto/ Shutterstock** (pp. 54–55, 58–59, all except Antarctica); **isak55/ Shutterstock** (p. 13); **Eric Isselee/Shutterstock** (p. 99); **Tomo Jesenicnik** (p. 69 right); **Joanna22/Shutterstock** (back cover, p. 3); **Kadak/Shutterstock** (p. 47); **Iakov Kalinin/Shutterstock** (p. 73); **Alex Kalmbach/Shutterstock** (p. 70); **Justin Kim/Shutterstock** (p. 97); **Marilyn D. Lambertz/Shutterstock** (p. 20 bottom); **libra/ Shutterstock** (p. 25 top); **Alta Oosthuizen/Shutterstock** (p. 96); **RHIMAGE/Shutterstock** (p. 116 bottom); **Dulce Rubia/ Shutterstock** (p. 121); **sagir/Shutterstock** (p. 69 left); **Schalke fotografie/Melissa Schalke/Shutterstock** (p. 92); **Dani Simmonds/ Shutterstock** (p. 32); **Andrea J Smith/Shutterstock** (p. 18 top); **spirit of america/Shutterstock** (p. 34); **SweetCrisis/Shutterstock** (p. 7 bottom); **tantrik71/Shutterstock** (pp. 115, 116 top); **Vector Shots/Shutterstock** (p. 16 top right); **Vibe Images/Shutterstock** (p. 63 top); **VoodooDot/Shutterstock** (p. 49); **yoolarts/Shutterstock** (p. 127).

**Some border icon art throughout courtesy of Shutterstock.**

Adventure awaits at
# MagicTreeHouse.com

# Track the Facts and Go on Adventures with Jack & Annie!

Join Jack and Annie on brand-new missions and play the Fact Tracker Showdown!

**Exclusive to You!**
Use this code to unlock additional journal activity pages!

REWARD CODE
EXPLORE

MAGIC TREE HOUSE®

RHCB

# Magic Tree House® Books

#1: Dinosaurs Before Dark
#2: The Knight at Dawn
#3: Mummies in the Morning
#4: Pirates Past Noon
#5: Night of the Ninjas
#6: Afternoon on the Amazon
#7: Sunset of the Sabertooth
#8: Midnight on the Moon
#9: Dolphins at Daybreak
#10: Ghost Town at Sundown
#11: Lions at Lunchtime
#12: Polar Bears Past Bedtime
#13: Vacation Under the Volcano
#14: Day of the Dragon King
#15: Viking Ships at Sunrise
#16: Hour of the Olympics
#17: Tonight on the *Titanic*
#18: Buffalo Before Breakfast
#19: Tigers at Twilight
#20: Dingoes at Dinnertime
#21: Civil War on Sunday
#22: Revolutionary War on Wednesday
#23: Twister on Tuesday
#24: Earthquake in the Early Morning
#25: Stage Fright on a Summer Night
#26: Good Morning, Gorillas
#27: Thanksgiving on Thursday
#28: High Tide in Hawaii

## Merlin Missions
#29: Christmas in Camelot
#30: Haunted Castle on Hallows Eve
#31: Summer of the Sea Serpent
#32: Winter of the Ice Wizard

#33: Carnival at Candlelight
#34: Season of the Sandstorms
#35: Night of the New Magicians
#36: Blizzard of the Blue Moon
#37: Dragon of the Red Dawn
#38: Monday with a Mad Genius
#39: Dark Day in the Deep Sea
#40: Eve of the Emperor Penguin
#41: Moonlight on the Magic Flute
#42: A Good Night for Ghosts
#43: Leprechaun in Late Winter
#44: A Ghost Tale for Christmas Time
#45: A Crazy Day with Cobras
#46: Dogs in the Dead of Night
#47: Abe Lincoln at Last!
#48: A Perfect Time for Pandas
#49: Stallion by Starlight
#50: Hurry Up, Houdini!
#51: High Time for Heroes
#52: Soccer on Sunday

# Magic Tree House® Fact Trackers

# More Magic Tree House®

# Read these books for even more Magic Tree House fun!